DOLPHINS

SPINNER DOLPHINS

JOHN F. PREVOST
ABDO & Daughters

Published by Abdo & Daughters, 4940 Viking Drive, Suite 622, Edina, Minnesota 55435.

Library bound edition distributed by Rockbottom Books, Pentagon Tower, P.O. Box 36036, Minneapolis, Minnesota 55435.

Printed in the United States.

Cover Photo credit: Peter Arnold, Inc.

Interior Photo credits: Peter Arnold, Inc.

Edited by Bob Italia

Library of Congress Cataloging-in-Publication Data

Prevost, John F.
  Spinner dolphins - by John F. Prevost.
    p.   cm. — (Dolphins)
Includes bibliographical references and index.
    ISBN 1-56239-497-5
l. Stenella longirostris—Juvenile literature. [l. Spinner dolphln. 2. Dolphins.]
I. Title. II. Series: Prevost, John F. Dolphins.
QL737.C432P745   1995
599.5'3--dc20   95-12368
                                                                   CIP
                                                                   AC

ABOUT THE AUTHOR

John Prevost is a marine biologist and diver who has been active in conservation and education issues for the past 18 years. Currently he is living inland and remains actively involved in freshwater and marine husbandry, conservation and education projects.

Contents

SPINNER DOLPHINS AND FAMILY

Spinner dolphins are small-toothed whales. Whales are **mammals**. They have some hair when born, are **warm blooded**, and make milk for their young. They are called spinners because they often spin when swimming and as they leap out of the water.

There are several different spinner dolphin groups. Many are divided by distance and **continents**. Spinner dolphins are also known as long-**snouted** dolphins. Relatives of the spinner dolphin are the spotted and striped dolphin.

Spinner dolphins get their name from the way they spin when swimming and leaping.

SIZE, SHAPE AND COLOR

Spinner dolphins are 5.4 to 7 feet (1.7 to 2.2 meters) long. Spinner dolphins differ in size and color. Males are slightly larger than females. In some Pacific groups males have a small hump below and in front of their **flukes**.

All spinner dolphins have slim bodies and long, thin **snouts**. Some groups may have longer or thinner snouts.

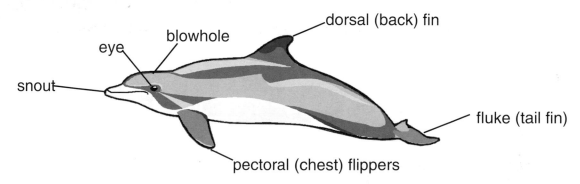

Most dolphins share the same features.

Spinner dolphins are marked by three bands of color.

Spinners are marked with three bands of color. Their backs are a dark gray. Their sides are a lighter gray or tan, and the underside is a cream or white. Some groups may have light spots on their bodies or dark markings on fins and **snouts**.

WHERE THEY LIVE

Spinner dolphins are found in the **tropical** and **sub-tropical** waters of the Atlantic, Pacific and Indian oceans. They are found less often in warm-**temperate** waters.

Spinners live near the ocean surface far from land. Only the Hawaiian and Costa Rican groups are often found close to shore. Spinners can dive 200 feet (61 meters) to find **prey**.

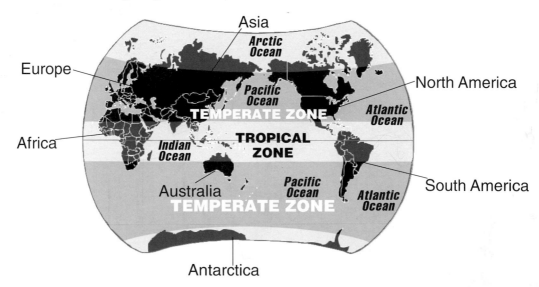

Spinner dolphins are often seen riding and jumping from the bow waves of ships.

Spinner dolphins are often seen riding and jumping from the **bow waves** of ships. They live in large **pods** of over 1,000 members. Often other dolphins and whales are with them. Pacific groups may travel with yellowfin tuna.

SENSES

Spinner dolphins and people have 4 of the same senses. Their eyesight is good and they can see well in or out of the water. Spinner dolphins are great jumpers and will often leap, spinning high above the water to look around.

Hearing is their most important sense. All toothed whales use **echolocation** to see underwater. They make a series of whistles and clicks, then listen to the returning echoes.

HOW ECHOLOCATION WORKS

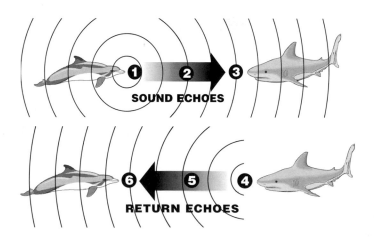

The dolphin sends out sound echoes (1). These echoes travel in all directions through the water (2). The sound echoes reach an object in the dolphin's path (3), then bounce off it (4). The return echoes travel through the water (5) and reach the dolphin (6). These echoes let the dolphin know where the object is, how large it is, and how fast it is moving.

Spinner dolphins are social animals that often touch each other as they swim.

Spinner dolphins are **social** animals. They often touch each other as they swim. This helps them to **communicate**. Spinners have a sense of taste, but lack the sense of smell.

DEFENSE

Large sharks, killer whales and man hunt spinner dolphins. Speed and quickness are their best defense. Its well-developed sense of hearing allows the **pod** to listen for danger and **communicate** warnings. Young dolphins and weak adults are the most likely **prey** for sharks and killer whales.

Purse-seine tuna nets are very dangerous for the spinners because the dolphins become trapped and cannot breathe. Unlike the common dolphins, spinners cannot escape and are often drowned in these nets. Recent changes in fishing laws and practices have lowered the number of spinners killed in tuna nets.

The spinner dolphin's best defense is to swim from danger.

FOOD

Spinner dolphins have 45 to 65 pairs of teeth in each jaw. These small, sharp teeth are made for gripping **prey**, not for cutting or tearing. Spinner dolphins feed on small fish and **squid** which are swallowed whole.

Spinners can dive deep to find prey. They often hunt at night. Dolphins find their prey using **echolocation**. To organize the hunt, spinners **communicate** underwater with each other using loud whistle sounds.

Spinner dolphins organize a hunt by communicating with loud whistles and sounds.

BABIES

A baby spinner dolphin is called a **calf**. At birth, a calf is 27.5 to 33.5 inches (70 to 85 centimeters) long. Like other **mammals**, the mother makes milk for her calf.

While the mother is feeding, the calf is left with other females. Males do not help with a calf. The "baby-sitters" are related to the mother. They keep the young dolphin safe. The calf will **nurse** for a year. It will not become an adult until it is 4 to 9 years old.

Other spinner dolphins will help the mother
"baby-sit" the calves.

SPINNER DOLPHIN FACTS

Scientific Name: *Stenella longirostris*
Synonyms, or scientific names of regional species now considered as *S. longirostris: S. microps, S. roseiventris, and S. longirostris kunitomoi.*

Average Size: 5.4 to 7 feet (1.7 to 2.2 meters) long. Males are often larger than females.

Where They're Found: In warm-**temperate** and **tropical** waters of the Atlantic, Pacific, and Indian oceans.

The spinner dolphin.

GLOSSARY

BOW WAVES - Waves pushed up by a ship's front.

CALF - A baby dolphin.

COASTAL - Bordering on water, shore.

COMMUNICATE (kuh-MEW-nih-kate) - To show feelings.

CONTINENTS (KAHN-tih-nents) - The seven great land masses on Earth. The continents are North America, South America, Africa, Asia, Europe, Australia, and Antarctica.

ECHOLOCATION (ek-oh-low-KAY-shun) - The use of sound waves to find objects underwater.

FLUKES - The tail of a whale.

MAMMAL - A group of warm-blooded animals that feed their young with milk from the mother's breast.

MIGRATE - To move from one place to another with the changing seasons.

NURSE - To give milk to the baby from the mother's breast.

POD - A herd or school of sea mammals.

PREY - Animals that are eaten by other animals.

PURSE-SEINE NETS - A fishing net used to trap tuna and other schooling fish, named for the large pocket that traps the fish as the nets are being pulled.

SNOUT - The protruding part on the front of an animal's face.

SOCIAL - Living in organized groups.

SQUID - Sea animals related to the octopus that are streamlined in shape and have at least ten arms.

SUB-TROPICAL - The region bordering the tropics.

TEMPERATE (TEM-prit) - The part of the Earth where the oceans are not very hot, or not very cold.

TROPICAL (TROP-ih-kul) - The part of the Earth near the equator where the oceans are very warm.

WARM-BLOODED - An animal whose body temperature remains the same and warmer than the outside air or water temperature.

Index

BIBLIOGRAPHY

Cousteau, Jacques-Yves. *The Whale, Mighty Monarch of the Sea.* N.Y.: Doubleday, 1972.

Dozier, Thomas A. *Whales and Other Sea Mammals.* Time-Life Films, 1977.

Leatherwood, Stephen. *The Sierra Club Handbook of Whales and Dolphins.* San Francisco, California: Sierra Club Books, 1983.

Minasian, Stanley M. *The World's Whales.* Washington, D.C.: Smithsonian Books, 1984.

Ridgway, Sam H., ed. *Mammals of the Sea.* Springfield, Illinois: Charles C. Thomas Publisher, 1972.